The Majesty of the Garden District

The Majesty of the
GARDEN DISTRICT

Photography by Paul Malone
Text by Lee Malone

PELICAN PUBLISHING COMPANY
Gretna 2004

First printing, 1994
Second printing, 1998
Third printing, 2004

We acknowledge with sincere appreciation the assistance, knowledge, and expertise from the following:

Michael M. Pilié
Louis and Joni Darré and the staff of Professional Color Service
Paul Ricalde
Eric Enright
The New Orleans Central Public Library, Louisiana Division
The Historic New Orleans Collection
Dr. Milburn and Nancy Calhoun and the staff of Pelican Publishing Company
The gracious Garden District homeowners

The word "Pelican" and the depiction of a pelican are trademarks
of Pelican Publishing Company, Inc.,
and are registered in the U.S. Patent and Trademark Office.

Library of Congress Cataloging-in-Publication Data

Malone, Paul.
　　The majesty of the Garden District / photography by Paul Malone ;
text by Lee Malone.
　　　　p.　cm.
　　Includes bibliographical references.
　　ISBN 1-56554-014-X
　　1. Dwellings—Louisiana—New Orleans. 2. Architecture, Domestic—
Louisiana—New Orleans. 3. Garden District (New Orleans, La.) 4. New Orleans
(La.)—Buildings, structures, etc. I. Malone, Lee.
　　II. Title.
　　NA7238.N5M36　1994
　　728.8'09763'35—dc20
　　　　　　　　　　　　　　　　　　　　　　　　　　　　　　93-41390
　　　　　　　　　　　　　　　　　　　　　　　　　　　　　　CIP

Photo on p. 2: This view of Pritchard-Pigott House's living room shows the marble fire-
place and the baby grand piano.
Photo on p. 8: The dining room of the Sweet-Uhalt House features a Henry Howard arch.
Photo on p. 10: Trinity Episcopal Church seems to invite one to enter and pray.

Book design by Dana Bilbray

Printed in Singapore

Published by Pelican Publishing Company, Inc.
1000 Burmaster Street, Gretna, Louisiana 70053

Contents

To the memory of Paul Malone,
my beloved husband, loyal companion, and friend,
who died shortly after this book was completed

Introduction

In 1816 a break in the levee at Macarty Plantation, located a few miles upriver in the town of Carrollton, caused the Mississippi River to inundate several plantations above New Orleans. This devastating flood left a thick layer of alluvial deposits over the vast Livaudais Plantation land located approximately four miles above the City of New Orleans. The combination of these deposits and the semitropical climate resulted in fertile soil, therefore promoting lush, verdant plant growth and an abundance of fragrant, colorful flowers. It also raised the ground level so that the result was better drainage of the land.

In 1825 the owners of the Livaudais Plantation, François de Livaudais and his wife, Celeste, were separated. Mrs. Livaudais received the plantation, among other properties, in the settlement. She moved to Paris and sold the plantation through her New Orleans attorneys.

The town of Lafayette was brought into being when the extensive Livaudais Plantation was divided into spacious lots and incorporated with two other New Orleans faubourgs (suburbs) in 1833. Construction of large, majestic homes was begun almost immediately. Each one was surrounded by flourishing gardens, featuring live oak, banana, palmetto, crepe myrtle, and magnolia trees.

The architects of homes built at that time, whatever architectural type, took into consideration the humid, warm climate of this region. The windows were large and many times situated opposite each other, creating cross-ventilation. Ceilings were high, so that the warmer air rose to the top of the rooms and the heavier cooler air was concentrated below. The rooms were large and airy. Many times the walls were fifteen inches thick, affording insulation from either summer or winter outdoor temperatures.

Of great importance was Toby's Corner (1838), which has been occupied by the Westfeldt family since 1858 when it was purchased after Thomas Toby's death. When the Toby-Westfeldt house was built on Prytania Street, construction activity shifted from the area near the river toward the transportation system with the coming of the railway down Nayades Street (now St. Charles Avenue).

In 1852 the area was annexed to New Orleans and became known as the Garden District because of its magnificent homes of varied architectural types, the towering trees, and the lovely, flowering gardens.

It is bounded by Jackson Avenue, Louisiana Avenue, Magazine Street, and St. Charles Avenue.

The Majesty of the Garden District

Harris-Maginnis-Schreiber House
2127 Prytania Street

In 1857-58, this imposing mansion was designed by James Calrow, who also served as builder with his partner, Mr. Day. It was erected for Alexander Harris, a cotton factor. John H. Maginnis purchased the home in 1871 for his family, who lived there for many years. From 1939 until 1954 it was the local headquarters for the American Red Cross. Dr. and Mrs. Clyde Crassons restored the lovely home in 1954 when they bought it.

Throughout the years the mansion changed ownership several times. It is now owned by Mr. and Mrs. Peter Schreiber, who are remodeling and renovating the graceful, symmetrical mansion. Elaborate, fluted Corinthian columns span the width of the house. Pilasters of the same design flank the entrance door. An iron-lace railing encircles the gallery.

Upon completion of restoration, Mr. and Mrs. Schreiber plan to convert this home into a charming, quaint bed and breakfast inn.

In the entrance hall, which is sixty-seven feet by twelve feet, one finds an antique French trumeau mirror over an antique console.

Through the rear door of the double parlor may be glimpsed the bright, cheerful breakfast room. Against the rear wall of the double parlor stands a black and gold mantelpiece of Italian marble, with a tall French mirror above it. Gold candlesticks on the mantel and an antique chandelier complete the picture.

Double sliding doors, original to the house, separate the parlors, which have identical marble mantelpieces. Note the harmonious simplicity of the cornice and the elegance of the pilasters, with Corinthian capitals, flanking the sliding doors.

One of the bedrooms ready for occupancy. The carved mantelpiece is original to the house.

Another view of the bedroom.

Henry Sullivan Buckner House
1410 Jackson Avenue

This stately mansion, built in Greek Revival style, is one of the largest in the Garden District. It was erected in 1856 by Lewis E. Reynolds, architect and builder, for Henry Sullivan Buckner.

Buckner's daughter and her husband, Cartwright Eustis, resided in this magnificent structure until it changed ownership in 1923. It then became the noted Soulé College until 1983.

The central hallway in the Buckner House is filled with Victorian furniture. Note the beautiful chandelier.

In the large dining room one finds an Italian marble mantelpiece, a long dining table on an antique rug, and two sparkling crystal chandeliers.

The front parlor has another Italian marble mantelpiece, an antique rug, a Victorian chandelier, and in the middle of the floor is a whimsical, Arabian antique chair and small table. They are both collapsible to allow convenient transportation by camelback.

Trinity Episcopal Church
1329 Jackson Avenue

At the corner of Jackson Avenue and Coliseum Street stands this imposing Gothic Revival-style church, which was built in 1852-53 by George Purves, architect-builder. In 1873 the present front and tower were planned and constructed by Charles L. Hilger, architect, and P. R. Middlemiss, builder.

Leonidas Polk became bishop of Louisiana in 1841 and in 1854 became affiliated with Trinity Church. During active service in the Confederate army, Polk was killed in Georgia in 1864 and was laid to rest in Christ Church Cathedral in New Orleans.

This glowing view of the interior of Trinity Episcopal Church shows the Gothic style of the arch leading into the altar area, and the beautifully arched ceiling.

Spectacular Gothic-style windows are featured along the side of the church.

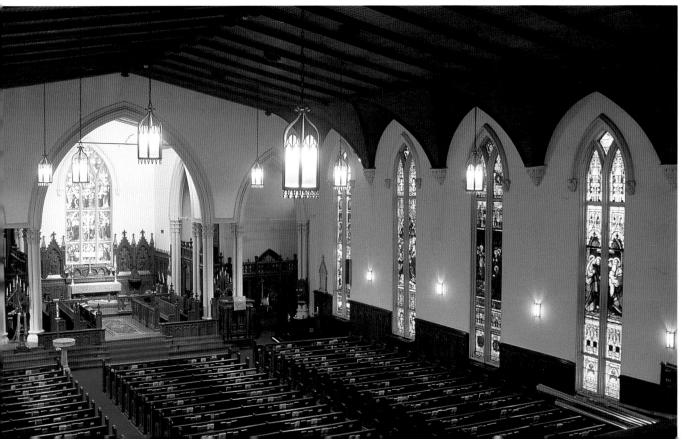

Sweet-Uhalt House
1236 Jackson Avenue

George O. Sweet commissioned Henry Howard, noted architect, to build this impressive home in 1874. Records indicate its completion in 1876. Sweet had originally purchased the lot with an existing house on it in 1852, but was not financially able to have this elegant, larger home built at that time.

The house is built in the Italianate style. Its plan is asymmetrical and complex, with a large semi-octagonal bay on the left side, a slightly recessed smaller one on the right side, and a projecting rear wing. A low-pitched, slate, hipped roof covers the remarkable structure.

Across the front part of the home are closely spaced full-length windows, creating a sense of openness and allowing a tremendous amount of light and air into the interior. A wide gallery practically surrounds the building. It runs in front of the right side wing, across the main facade, turns the corner at the left side, then wraps around the large bay to terminate in the rear. It has no balustrade but is enclosed by chamfered wooded box columns that sit on simple, short newel-posts. A modified segmental arch motif is formed by slightly arched wooden panels inserted between the columns. The floor of the gallery has an inlaid marble design, with carved marble stairs leading up to the front door. The building's cornice is deep, with small attic-level ventilators in it.

The spacious, beautifully landscaped grounds enhance this lovely Garden District home.

After the original owner's death, ownership changed several times. The present owner, Hugh C. Uhalt, is constantly improving both the interior and exterior of this magnificent mansion.

This view of the living room shows the crystal chandelier hanging from a beautiful ceiling medallion, the carved mantelpiece, and a painting by Edward M. Hall, dated 1885, entitled In the Days of Phidias.

Henry Howard, architect, was known for his use of decorative archways. In this view of the master bedroom one sees the master bed through an archway that is similar to one that Howard designed for Nottoway Plantation Home. To the left one looks into the hand-painted central hall.

Library showing Henry Howard arches on both sides of the glowing room.

This view shows two Howard arches; one at the end of the entrance hall, and the other at the end of the rear hall. The window looks out at the beautiful garden.

The magnificent dining-room mantelpiece carved with griffins. The painting is by the original school of Sir Peter Lily.

Guest bedroom with a view of the semi-octagonal bay and the lovely French antique bedroom set adorned with ormolu. Above the bed is a painting by Franz M. Melchers, entitled Mountain Nymphs, *1925.*

The upstairs central hall, with spectacular hand-painted walls, shows an antique French Provincial wrought-iron console table under a painting by Roland Monachiem.

The beautifully landscaped, colorful rear yard is peaceful.

Hobson-Haack House
1224 Jackson Avenue

In approximately 1860, near the beginning of the Civil War, this captivating raised cottage was built. The architect is believed to be the noted Henry Howard.

Seven fluted Corinthian columns span the width of the house. The ironwork railing has a beautiful pattern of lyres and flowers. On the left side of the central doorway is a lovely bay.

The interior is furnished with French and English antiques. The present owners collected blue and white porcelain when they lived in the Middle East and in India.

The house was bought by John and Ann Hobson in 1962 and their five children were reared here. It is now owned by John Hobson's widow, Ann, and her husband, Frederick Haack.

The living room is light and airy. A Louis XVI-style bronze-doré chandelier hangs from a beautiful ceiling medallion, which is in a delicate, flower design. Note the Dutch walnut secretary, ca. 1740, and the pair of Louis XVI chairs.

Another view of the living room features the nine-teenth-century white Italian marble mantelpiece with central cartouche, and the Italian rococo mirror of giltwood. On each side of the mantel is a Chinese-export ginger jar.

The dining room features a crystal and bronze-doré Louis XVI-style chandelier and another Italian marble mantelpiece. On the Georgian oval, three-part dining table there are English silver candlesticks and a silver swan on an English silver plateau.

This is a view of the remarkable spiral staircase, which seems to defy gravity.

A tranquil part of the garden.

Colorful flowers beginning to bloom in early spring.

Goldsmith-Sheen House
1122 Jackson Avenue

Henry Howard, noted nineteenth-century architect, designed this impressive residence in 1859-60 for Manuel Goldsmith. The land had been part of the Rousseau Plantation located in Faubourg Lafayette.

Throughout the years the stately home changed hands several times until the present owners, Dr. and Mrs. Alan E. Sheen, purchased it in 1975. They have meticulously restored the beautiful old home to its original elegance. When Dr. Sheen researched the house he came across every handwritten document by the architect, Henry Howard. He knew, therefore, where every window, door, etc., was or was not supposed to be.

Ninety percent of the fresco paintings in the ballroom are original. After layers of paint were removed, only 10 percent had to be retouched. Over this there are five coats of sealer. Fresco is wet paint applied to the last layer of plaster so that it is sealed into the walls.

This magnificent ballroom is one of three original ballrooms still in existence in the Garden District.

The entrance hallway is a dramatic introduction to the spectacular mansion. The hall table is Italian Renaissance and has been in the family for four generations. Cuban mahogany was used for the stair railing. Note the Venetian chandelier and the beautiful medallion.

An overall view of the magnificent ballroom. Note the frescoed ceiling, the medallion, the gilded archway, and the warm, welcoming glow. Along the walls one sees Hepplewhite chairs, ca. 1770. In this room many notable guests were entertained.

AT LEFT: This view of the house shows the rear wing.

The dining-room table is of highly polished mahogany and is surrounded by Hepplewhite chairs.

In the living room the fireplace is made of iron with faux marble. Note the French chandelier.

Photographed from the front gate, looking into the garden, the Alhambra fountain with arching jets of water creates a soothing atmosphere.

This lovely, colorful garden is laid out exactly as it was originally.

St. Mary's Assumption Roman Catholic Church
2052 Constance Street

The first Roman Catholic church in the Lower Garden District was built on this site in 1843 by the Redemptorist Fathers and the German-speaking Catholics in the area.

Archbishop Antoine Blanc laid the cornerstone of the present magnificent German baroque brick structure on April 25, 1858. Dedication took place on June 24, 1860.

Father Francis Xavier Seelos, C.S.S.R. was laid to rest beneath the sanctuary when he died of yellow fever while attending to victims of the 1867 epidemic.

In 1965 the church was extensively damaged by Hurricane Betsy. It was restored to its original splendor in 1975.

Rising from the rear of the church is an exceptionally remarkable 142-foot tower. The lower part is square, the second part is octagon-shaped, and then the top ascends gracefully.

The interior of the church seems to glow. Lights outline the main altar. Fluted Corinthian columns and pilasters support a beautifully arched ceiling. Gold leaf on plaster is used lavishly as decoration in this majestic old church.

Lavinia C. Dabney House
2265 St. Charles Avenue

Lavinia C. Dabney engaged Gallier, Turpin, and Company to build this Garden District mansion in 1856-57. It was the residence of the Jonas O. Rosenthal family from 1893 to 1952. From 1952 to 1972 it was occupied as the diocesan house of the Episcopal Diocese of Louisiana.

Grinnan-Reily House
2221 Prytania Street

Robert A. Grinnan, an Englishman, commissioned Henry Howard, architect, to design this beautiful mansion in 1850. The builder was John Sewell.

Howard designed several of the majestic homes in the New Orleans area. The entrance-door motif is similar to the crest he designed for Nottoway, the impressive plantation home located in White Castle, Louisiana.

Delgado-Rice House
1220 Philip Street

This exquisite mansion was built for Mrs. Augustin Marius Tureaud in the late 1850s. It is constructed entirely of wood and is typical of houses built just before the Civil War. Both upper and lower galleries have fluted Corinthian columns, with ironwork railings on the upper gallery. The upper portions of windows and shutters are gracefully carved. A semi-octagonal bay is on the north side of the house. The rear north wing has now been converted into a separate, charming "maisonette" (small house). At an auction in 1866, Trinity Episcopal Church bought the lovely house for use as a rectory; however, it was sold again in 1868 to Samuel and Sarah Delgado.

Samuel Delgado, a wealthy sugar and molasses broker, and his wife were childless and took their fourteen-year-old nephew, Isaac Delgado, from Jamaica into their home. Though the boy was young, he had great business expertise and soon entered the world of commerce. In a few years he began amassing a fortune and this beautiful residence housed his art collection, which later became the nucleus of our city's art museum.

Many years before his death, Isaac Delgado, a bachelor, gave away huge sums. His art collection and $150,000 were donated to erect the Delgado Museum of Art in City Park. Because of illness he was unable to attend the dedication ceremonies in 1911. This greatly disappointed him. When he died in 1912, he bequeathed his home to the city and left his millions for hospitals and the trade school that bears his name.

This majestic home served as the British Consulate for a brief time, and then it was sold to David Pipes. The present owners, Mr. and Mrs. Atwood Rice, Jr., purchased the house in 1972. They carefully and lovingly preserve their delightful home.

In the entrance hallway one sees a crystal chandelier, an antique console table, and the beautiful, mahogany staircase.

The front parlor features a Colonial-style sofa flanked by Colonial-style mahogany tables, a carved marble mantelpiece with a French mirror, and an antique epergne on the mantel.

An identical marble mantelpiece with an identical French mirror graces the back parlor. By the window stands a small Duncan Phyfe table. In front of the sofa one finds a charming English tea table. In this view can be seen the spectacular carved arch separating the parlors.

In the dining room is a Georgian mahogany sideboard with an antique French mirror, original to the house, a silver service, and silver candelabra.

The marble mantelpiece in the dining room is original to the house. Above the Georgian mahogany table and chairs hangs a crystal chandelier from an exquisite medallion.

The cheerful dining room of the maisonette.

The living room of the maisonette features a marble mantelpiece with a French mirror above it.

What a lovely garden in which to have breakfast on a sunny morning!

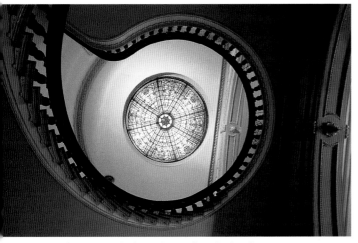

Bradish Johnson House
2343 Prytania Street

In 1872 this superb mansion was built for Bradish Johnson, a notable Louisiana sugar planter. Attributed to James Freret, architect, the design reflects the influence of the French Ecole des Beaux Arts, where he studied from 1860 to 1862.

The family of Walter Denegre acquired ownership in 1892 and remained in residence until 1929 when it changed hands and became the Louise S. McGehee School.

The stained-glass dome floods the three-story stairway with soft light. As the sun sinks lower in the sky, the light from the dome becomes golden.

As one steps into the entrance hall, one is impressed by the grandeur of the elaborate cornice work and the delicate beauty of the curving stairway.

Elaborately carved cornices and a striking medallion are seen in the room across from the staircase.

A view of the house showing its surrounding foliage.

Toby's Corner
2340 Prytania Street

This comfortable home is believed to be the oldest in the Garden District. It was built at the edge of the Livaudais Plantation in 1838 for Thomas Toby. It is located at the corner of First and Prytania streets, hence the name *Toby's Corner.*

Toby was a Philadelphia businessman who came to this city in the early 1800s and made his fortune as a wheelwright. After Toby's death, the house was purchased in 1858 by Thomas Dugan as a wedding present to his daughter, Louise, who married into the Westfeldt family. Their descendants are still in residence.

Spacious, landscaped grounds surround the house, which is raised on brick piers. This type of architecture reflects the style of the West Indies plantation homes built at that time.

A large bookcase takes up almost all of one wall in the parlor. The center alcove contains a lovely portrait of Mary Scott Phillips, wife of Dr. Willam D. Phillips, grandfather of Thomas Dugan Westfeldt II. Above two black Italian marble mantelpieces, one on each side of the bookcase, one finds a portrait of each of Mr. and Mrs. Westfeldt's little girls.

Close-up of one of the Italian marble mantelpieces, all of which were originally pinewood until replacement before the turn of the century.

In the corner of the parlor stands an antique music box made in Switzerland.

At the top of the stairs, under a beautiful crystal chandelier, one finds an unusual, antique upright baby grand piano. This type of baby grand piano was manufactured for a short period of time by Rippen Manufacturing Company.

Carroll-Brown House
1315 First Street

Designed and built in 1869 by Samuel Jamison, this spectacular mansion has many elaborate Italianate features. Joseph Carroll, a Virginian who became one of the most successful cotton factors in the city, was its first owner.

The present owners are Dr. and Mrs. Morton Brown.

Pritchard-Pigott House
1407 First Street

In 1858 Richard Pritchard, a wealthy cotton factor, bought this site from attorney Robert N. Ogden. He commissioned the architectural firm of Howard and Diettel to draw the plans and execute the building of this imposing mansion.

After the Civil War the house changed ownership several times.

The house was shown on the Braun map, 1874, in its original, smaller configuration with a full-width front gallery. An *L*-shaped rear addition with a gallery and another gallery on the Coliseum side of the house were shown on the 1887 Sanborn map.

In 1904 the home was purchased and renovated by Emmet and John Hinton, giving it a Renaissance Revival appearance. A New Orleans newspaper reported that Soulé and MacDonnell were the architects for this work.

The present owners, Dr. and Mrs. John Pigott, restored this impressive mansion to its original splendor.

Four immense fluted columns support the deep, heavy entablature.

Delicate peach-colored accents are found in the dining room. Chippendale chairs surround the table. The carved, wooden mantelpiece has marble around the fireplace grate. The antique rug is a Turkish Oushak.

The bright, cheerful entrance hall has a luminous quality. Note the spectacular stair-way and balcony.

One finds dark, carved mahogany woodwork in the comfortable library.

The lovely and tranquil living room sets the happy, welcoming mood of the house. Note the intricately carved cornice and ceiling ornamentation.

Morris-Israel-Aron House
1331 First Street

Construction of this stately home was begun in 1860 by Samuel Jamison, architect. Building was delayed by the Civil War and was not completed until 1868. The house was sold approximately one year later to Joseph C. Morris, whose family occupied it until 1921. For the next six years this lovely home was a boardinghouse owned by a Mrs. McCraney. It was then purchased and restored by Dr. Ralph Hopkins, whose family lived there until 1967.

Mr. and Mrs. Sam Israel, Jr., who became the owners in 1967, began the task of restoring the home to its original magnificence. The room that was the library is now the dining room. In this room five layers of wallpaper and paint were removed from the ceiling with extraordinary care. Thus, the full beauty of the original ceiling mural was revealed. The colors were amazingly fresh; however, there was minor damage, which was rectified by artist Vera Reinike, a muralist.

The exterior of the mansion is embellished by delicate iron lace, and as it stands today it is magnificent.

The present owners are Mr. and Mrs. Jack R. Aron, who lovingly preserve this impressive home.

The massive front door was carved in New Orleans by an Italian or French carver. It contains some designs that are duplicated in the marble mantelpieces, dining-room ceiling, medallions, etc., throughout the house.

Detail of the delicate iron lace.

Detail of the medallion, chandelier, and parlor cornice.

The double parlor has twin marble mantelpieces, crystal chandeliers, an Aubusson rug thought to be 200 years old, and an elaborately carved arch dividing the parlors. At the far side of the room is an exquisite portrait of Mrs. Aron painted by John Howard Sandon.

The dining room has a full pedestal table of Georgian mahogany, and twelve Chippendale chairs, ca. 1730, bought in England. The mirror and gold-leaf cornices are original to the house. The cornices were extended so that swags could be used. Note the spectacular mural on the ceiling.

The fountain in the beautiful garden is made of Italian carved stone.

Eighteenth- or nineteenth-century statues of little people, probably Austrian or Spanish, line the edge of a bed of colorful flowers.

Brevard-Mmahat-Rice House
1239 First Street

In 1857 this imposing Greek Revival house was erected for Albert Hamilton Brevard by James H. Calrow and Charles Pride. In 1869 the splendid home was bought by Emory Clapp, who added a library wing. It was the Clapp family residence until 1935. Since then ownership of the house has changed several times.

The Garden District

1 Harris-Maginnis-Schreiber House
2 Henry Sullivan Buckner House
3 Trinity Episcopal Church
4 Sweet-Uhalt House
5 Hobson-Haack House
6 Goldsmith-Sheen House
7 St. Mary's Assumption Roman Catholic Church
8 Lavinia C. Dabney House
9 Grinnan-Reily House
10 Delgado-Rice House
11 Bradish Johnson House
12 Toby's Corner
13 Carroll-Brown House
14 Pritchard-Pigott House
15 Morris-Israel-Aron House
16 Brevard-Mmahat-Rice House
17 Jacob U. Payne House
18 Adams House
19 Jane Schlesinger House
20 Joseph Merrick Jones House
21 Maddox-Mclendon House
22 New Orleans Opera Association—Women's Guild

23 Williams-Ordemann House
24 Terry-Rinehart House
25 Walter Grinnan Robinson Mansion
26 Musson-Bell House
27 Montgomery-Hero-Reynoir House
28 Hogan-Breit House
29 Koch-Brennan House
30 Hermann-Ballard House
31 Col. Robert H. Short Villa
32 Domingos House
33 Commander's Palace Tower
34 Lafayette Cemetery No. 1
35 Christ Church Cathedral
36 Dominique Stella House
37 McDermott-Laborde House
38 Van Benthuysen-Elms House
39 George Washington Cable House
40 Thomas N. Bernard House

Off map:
41 Morris Mansion
42 Stewart House
43 Alfred Grima House

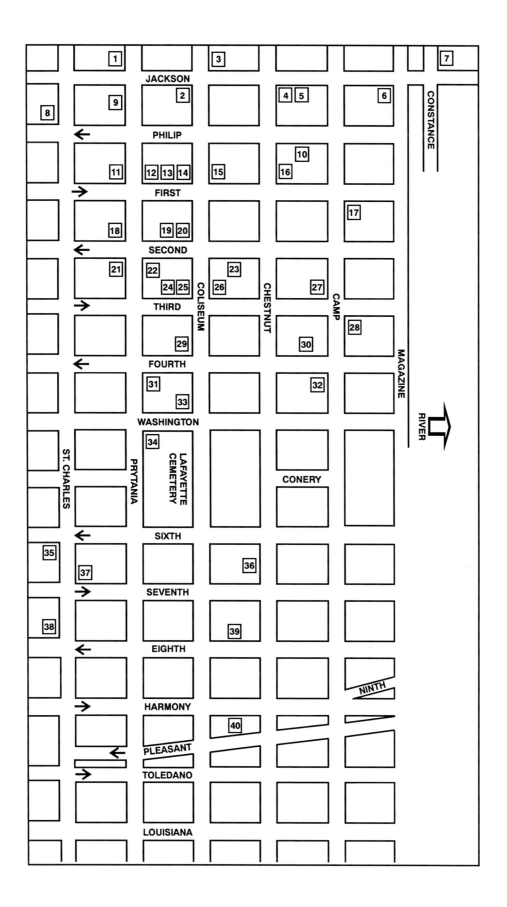

Jacob U. Payne House
1134 First Street

In 1849-50 this impressive home was built for Jacob U. Payne. Its galleries span the width of the house with Ionic columns on the lower floor and Tower of the Winds capitals topping the columns on the second floor.

The Payne family occupied the stately mansion for several years. Later, Judge Charles Erasmus Fenner, Payne's son-in-law and close friend of Jefferson Davis, lived here. Jefferson Davis was a guest of the Fenner family when he died on December 6, 1889.

Ownership was retained by later members of the family until it was sold in 1935 to Mr. and Mrs. William Bradish Forsyth, the parents of Mrs. Frank Strachan, the present owner.

In this room, located at the rear of the main-floor hallway, Confederate President Jefferson Davis died. This is not the original furniture.

In the entrance hallway one finds the original, carved staircase.

As one enters the hall, to the right is the parlor. The mantelpiece is of coral on Belgian marble and is original to the house. The chandelier is of Baccarat crystal. English Georgian furniture fills the warm, welcoming room.

The living room is opposite the parlor. In the lower left of the photograph is a display of keepsakes from the day Mr. Frank Strachan ruled as Rex, king of Mardi Gras. Above the fireplace hangs a lovely portrait of Mrs. Frank Strachan, which was painted by German artist Leon Kroll.

A flowering archway leads into the formal garden.

A view of the formal garden with the tea house in the rear.

Adams House
2423 Prytania Street

In 1860 this stately home was erected for John I. Adams, merchant. He purchased this part of the former plantation of François de Livaudais and made it his residence until 1896.

It is believed to have been designed by Frederick Wing.

The comfortable, lovely home changed ownership several times throughout the years. The present owners, who purchased it in 1972, are preserving it splendidly.

Jane Schlesinger House
1427 Second Street

Jane Fawcett, James D'Arcy's widow, purchased this site in 1845. The house is presumed to be a part of a large plantation home. In the early 1850s this part was moved to this location and additions were built. The architect is not known.

Several architectural features are those of houses built at that time: the twelve-foot-high ceilings, the single-width doors, and the door moldings, which are the same pattern as those in the Pontalba buildings. The floor plan is typi-cal of houses built in the 1850s. The central hall is flanked by spacious rooms.

This stately mansion's facade has floor to ceiling windows, Corinthian columns connected by iron railings on the lower gallery, and Ionic columns connected by iron railings on the upper gallery. A beautifully designed entablature is topped by a parapet.

The present owner, Jane M. Schlesinger, and her three children have been in residence since 1974.

The staircase, giving access to the second floor, is of highly polished mahogany.

Above the carved marble mantelpiece in the parlor hangs an ancestor's portrait. Note the cornice work and the sliding doors.

This view of the dining room shows a carved wood mantelpiece with marble around the fireplace.

A relaxing area outside of the sun-room.

The circular brick planter on the terrace features a Venetian urn in the center.

Joseph Merrick Jones House
2425 Coliseum Street

This majestic old home was built in 1850 in the Greek Revival style of architecture. The additional wing at the side of the house was added at a later date.

The wide center hall, flanked by large, spacious rooms, is typical of houses built in that era.

Close-up of cast-iron gate and entrance doorway.

Maddox-Mclendon House
2507 Prytania Street

Joseph H. Maddox, owner of the New Orleans *Daily Crescent,* a noted newspaper at that time, purchased the square of land at the corner of Prytania and Second streets in June 1852. He commissioned John Barnett, architect, to draw the plans for his new residence. A contract for construction was signed with John R. Eichelberger in August. Edward Gotthiel, architect, was employed to supervise the construction.

Shortly after the house's completion, Maddox was embroiled in a ruinous lawsuit. The residence was seized by the sheriff and sold to John Coleman. Throughout the years ownership changed several times until it was bought in 1984 by Mrs. G. N. Mclendon, who has refurbished this magnificent mansion and furnished it with authentic antiques.

The entrance hall's floor is of polished pine. Cypress, walnut, and mahogany were all used in the gracefully winding staircase. The walls extending up the staircase were hand-painted by Vera Reinike, a famous artist.

The parlor walls are covered with rose fabric. The mantelpiece of burled walnut is matched by the parlor's sliding doors. Above the mantel is a French beveled mirror within a rare antique frame of six-inch thickness of molded porcelain in spectacular designs of flowers and bows with a cherub at the top.

Close-up of the ballroom's elaborate cornice, full archway, and both columns.

The mansion is famous for its opulent ballroom. It is nearly fifty feet long and has twin Baccarat chandeliers, two Italian marble fireplaces, and draped windows that rise from the floor to the extravagantly carved cornice. There is so much gilt along the walls and ceiling that it is known as the Gold Room. The archway curves gracefully above gilded Corinthian columns. The oak floor is designed for dancers, with boards laid diagonally for dramatic effect. In the left corner one sees a Venetian "blackamoor." This is a wood-carved Nubian figure with gilt drapery at the waist.

The unusual Italian lacquered secretary is of museum quality. The upper section is crowned by an arched bonnet with gilt, carved scroll flourishes. The lower section has a slanted front writing surface opening to reveal drawers within.

In the pool area, lush, verdant plants and colorful flowers abound.

New Orleans Opera Association—Women's Guild
2504 Prytania Street

This magnificent home was constructed for Edward Davis in 1858. It changed ownership several times until it was purchased by Dr. and Mrs. Herman de Bacchelle Seebold in 1944. They were both patrons of the arts.

Mrs. Seebold was a dedicated member of the New Orleans Opera Association's Women's Guild and when she died in 1966 she willed the house and its contents to the Guild.

The original section of the house is Greek Revival. In the late 1800s an addition was built in Italianate style. The Seebolds purchased many of the fixtures and furnishings in Europe during their travels.

With loving care the elegant old mansion has been beautifully preserved by the Women's Guild of the New Orleans Opera Association.

Note the entrance hall's elaborate plasterwork (friezes) and the beautiful beveled leaded-glass entrance doors. Flanking the hall are two antique tables with petticoat mirrors.

Note the hand-painted ceiling, intricately carved medallion, and cornice.

The front parlor features an Italian marble mantelpiece. Above the mantel one finds a mid-nineteenth-century mirror with gilt and lacquer in Louis XV style.

In the back parlor stands a twin Italian marble mantelpiece and a twin chandelier made of fire crystal and gilt. These twin chandeliers are from the Imperial Palaces in old St. Petersburg, Russia. The rug is French.

A magnificent crystal chandelier hangs in this room, which is opposite the double parlor.

An impressive, large old mahogany china cabinet stands in another room opposite the double parlor. It is elaborately carved.

The garden is filled with flowering plants. These are azaleas.

A cast-iron fence encloses the house.

Williams-Ordemann House
1320 Second Street

One of the loveliest homes in the Garden District is now owned by Ed and Susan Ordemann, who purchased it on February 7, 1992.

This magnificent structure was built in the late 1860s by Mary Anne Williams, widow of Mr. Louis Ogier. The architect is not known.

It is constructed of cypress wood, as so many homes were during that time. The lower-floor gallery curves gracefully and has slender cypress columns supporting the gallery roof. A cypress railing, of beautiful design, connects the columns. The second-floor balcony is identical in design. At the side of the house there is an attractive bay, which is topped by a lofty spire.

Throughout the years, this majestic home has changed ownership several times. The present owners maintain it carefully and lovingly.

Detail of railing and columns.

The entrance hallway, showing the elegant cypress staircase, the ceiling medallion and chandelier, the stained-glass windows, and the cypress mantelpiece with marble surrounding the fireplace.

This piano was built in the 1860s in England for Prince Albert. It bears the seal of the royal family.

The light, airy dining room has a crystal chandelier hanging from a ceiling medallion. Note the antique sideboard and the gleaming mahogany table, which were restored after a fire.

The glowing bay section of the living room showing the mirror above the mantelpiece. It is a French beveled mirror that was originally used on a river-boat about the turn of the century. After World War II it was gilded by a German immigrant.

In the bay section of the bedroom one finds a charming brass and iron bed. The night-stands and the trunk are antique.

Terry-Rinehart House
1417 Third Street

This was originally a small, charming carriage house in the rear of the large, main house, which was built in 1853 and faced Prytania Street. According to Samuel Wilson, Jr.'s *Guide to Architecture of New Orleans, 1699-1959,* the original architect and builder was Isaac Thayer.

Dr. and Mrs. Thomas M. Terry purchased the carriage house in the 1930s and commissioned Douglass Freret to direct a plan to preserve the interesting features of the house while adding modern accommodations, such as a swimming pool, an elevator, and a formal garden. The original exterior walls of the carriage house are thirteen inches thick and the broad doors, which once swung back to allow the passage of carriages, have been preserved.

Mr. and Mrs. Alan G. Rinehart bought the house and began extensive remodeling in 1976.

Walter Grinnan Robinson Mansion
1415 Third Street

One of the largest and most elegant mansions in the Garden District was built for Walter Grinnan Robinson in the late 1850s. Robinson came from Virginia to live in New Orleans.

The upper and lower galleries feature decorative rounded ends, a design often used by James Gallier, Sr., and James Gallier, Jr. Four majestic columns and two pilasters were used on each gallery. The massive entablature has an ornamental parapet.

Musson-Bell House
1331 Third Street

In 1850 Michel Musson, a wealthy cotton factor and postmaster of New Orleans, purchased the site on which this stately mansion stands. James Gallier, Sr., is said to have been commissioned to design the prepossessing home, which changed ownership in 1869.

Mr. Musson was the uncle of Edgar Degas, the French impressionist painter. In 1872 Edgar and his brother, René, came from France to visit their uncle and aunt and their four children, one of whom, Estelle, had been blind since the age of twelve. René and Estelle fell in love but were first cousins; however, they were able to obtain a dispensation from the Pope so that they could be married. Four children were born during this seemingly happy marriage. Estelle's best friend came to read to her in the afternoons and also flirted with René. Eventually the two of them ran away and Estelle was left with the children. Mr. Musson was so enraged that he adopted the four children, giving them his name and obliterating what was to become the famous Degas name. Edgar painted a portrait of his beautiful blind cousin. This painting of Estelle now hangs in our New Orleans Museum of Art.

In 1869 the house was sold to James Buckner, who in turn sold it to Charles M. Whitney in 1884. Many alterations were made to the house by Mr. Whitney. The front of the house had two bay windows with canopies over the two windows and the door. These were stripped off and galleries surrounded by delicate iron lace were added.

This magnificent Italianate-style mansion is now preserved by the present owners, Mr. and Mrs. Bryan Bell.

A crystal chandelier lights the foyer, in which one finds a gracefully curved, seemingly unsupported staircase and a Federal-style sofa.

In the living room this sitting arrangement is in front of a white marble mantelpiece in Louis XVI style. Note the elaborate plaster cornices. They are called "double transparencies" because they are set out at a slight angle from the wall.

Close-up of the living room's magnificent crystal chandelier.

A view of the sitting arrangement in the living-room bay window.

This room has always been used as the dining room despite the appearance of a drawing room. The two black marble mantelpieces are original to the house. The rose-colored bronze chandeliers were originally for gaslight; however, Mrs. Whitney had every other gas jet wired for electricity. The remaining gas jets have been convenient for gaslit dinners and when a power failure or a hurricane occurs. The portraits above the mantels are of Mr. and Mrs. Bell, painted by a German post-impressionist painter, Frederick Roscher.

The garden room is light, airy, and inviting.

Montgomery-Hero-Reynoir House
1213 Third Street

On a shady, tree-lined street in the Garden District stands this breathtaking mansion. It is believed to have been built by Archibald Montgomery prior to 1868, possibly before the Civil War. James Gallier, Jr., noted architect, is presumed to be the builder. Gothic-style moldings, slender columns, and sturdy balustrades all enhance the overall magnificence of the exterior.

The grounds are entered through an artistic iron gate. The gate and the fence are completely covered by a dense cherry-laurel hedge. The walk is paved with imported German flagstones, with lush, verdant plants and colorful flowers on each side. The stairs leading to the gallery are flanked by old-fashioned sweet olive trees.

One enters a welcoming vestibule leading into a spacious hall, which extends through the center of the house and opens into the rear yard. Large, airy rooms with fourteen-foot-high ceilings are on both sides of the hall.

In 1885, upon Mr. Montgomery's death, Mrs. Montgomery sold her lovely home to the Hero family, who held ownership until 1977.

The mansion has now been completely restored by the present owners, Mr. and Mrs. Gus Reynoir, who gave the home new life when they purchased it in February of 1978.

In an alcove at the right of the hall is a magnificent winding stairway, which has an elaborate, carved mahogany balustrade and is lighted by a yellow pivot window.

The inviting entrance hall is lighted by a crystal chandelier.

The grand drawing room, at the left of the hallway, extends from the front to the rear of the house. It is light and airy, partly because of the tall, undraped windows and doors, which are from floor to cornice.

To the right of the hallway an antique, carved wooden mantelpiece and a crystal chandelier grace the elegant parlor.

A circular pond with a fountain in the center of the garden. One sees rosebushes enclosed by a meticulously clipped hedge.

The garden's atmosphere is serene.

Hogan-Breit House
1138 Third Street

The two lots on which this majestic mansion stands were sold to Willis H. Hogan, a wealthy cotton factor, on April 12, 1869. Construction began, and the house was completed and occupied by 1870. It was the residence of the Hogan family for many years. In 1888 the lovely home was sold to Benjamin Franklin Eshleman by Miss Annie Watt Hogan.

Subsequent changes in ownership took place until Mr. and Mrs. Hjalmar E. Breit purchased the home on August 30, 1954. They immediately restored it to its original splendor and still preserve this stately mansion with loving care.

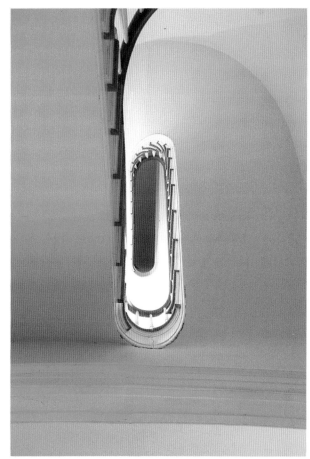

The gracefully curving staircase, with its mahogany railing and cypress treads, rises to the third floor.

Another view of the spectacular staircase. This is from the second floor.

In the double parlor, the mantelpiece is of marble. Above the mantel hangs a tall, antique mirror that reaches the intricately carved cornice. The crystal chandelier is imported.

The fireplace in the back parlor is of Italian marble, black with gold.

This is an antique Sheraton breakfront. It is approximately two hundred years old and was bought in Edinburgh, Scotland.

Note the elegance of the Chippendale chairs, the French oak sideboard, and the gleaming dining table. The rose-colored walls lend a warm glow.

The sideboard in the dining room.

This unusual round, gilt mirror reflects the staircase.

A lovely modern pool dresses up the landscaped yard.

Koch-Brennan House
2627 Coliseum Street

This fascinating "Swiss chalet"-style villa was built during the 1860s and reflects the picturesque taste of that time. The exterior of the house has elaborate scrollwork and cast-iron ornamentation, both of which enhance the irregular massing of many gables and galleries.

The interior of this lovely mansion is filled with beautiful antiques and the gardens are delightful.

Richard B. Eustis, ambassador to France, resided here from 1886 to 1903. The family of Richard Koch, architect, subsequently owned the mansion until 1953.

The present owners are Mr. and Mrs. Owen E. Brennan, who purchased it in 1969. It was restored at that time and is currently maintained with the utmost care.

The warm and welcoming entrance hallway has a staircase of walnut painted white. Family portraits hanging on the walls are family treasures. Note the stained-glass window at the rear and the "shadow" cornice work, which is perforated so that the juncture of wall and ceiling can be seen.

In the parlor the marble mantelpiece is original to the house. Hanging above the mantel is a trumeau mirror. The chandelier is Baccarat and the antique furniture is French.

A Baccarat chandelier hangs from a unique wooden medallion in the dining room. The cornice is also of wood, instead of plaster.

This was a double parlor that has been converted into a chapel where a Catholic Mass is held every other Wednesday throughout the year.

Part of the garden framed by iron lace, which encircles the gallery.

A spectacular view of the garden surrounding the pool.

Hermann-Ballard House
1227 Fourth Street

On March 28, 1844, Louis Florian Hermann purchased a whole square of land that had originally belonged to the vast Livaudais Plantation. Two days later he borrowed $3,000 from the Bank of Louisiana. Apparently, the loan was made in order to finance the building of this lovely, comfortable home.

The house faced Third Street at that time and occupied the whole square. This square was sold by Hermann in 1850 to Edward Ogden, who subdivided it. The superb residence was moved so that it faced Fourth Street.

In 1967, when the kitchen was enlarged, there was an opportunity to see the interior construction, which is heavy-timber framed, with mortise and tenon joints and wooden pegs. Much heavy cross bracing was used.

Throughout the years, ownership changed several times. The present owners, Mr. and Mrs. Westervelt T. Ballard, take pride in maintaining this impressive example of early Garden District architecture.

The warm glow of the entrance hall with the sparkling crystal chandelier hanging over an antique round table creates a tranquil atmosphere.

The tastefully furnished formal parlor is accented by lush green plants and a delicate orchid.

Above the black Italian marble mantelpiece one finds candelabra and a beveled mirror.

The beautifully curved staircase was originally outside of the house; however, the rear gallery has now been made into a charming sun-room.

114

The living room is comfortably appointed.

Yellow lilies in the landscaped garden.

Col. Robert H. Short Villa
Favrot House
1448 Fourth Street

Colonel Short's villa, now the Favrot House, was built in 1859 for Col. Robert H. Short of Kentucky. Henry Howard was the architect and Robert Huyhe was the builder.

On September 1, 1863, the Federal forces occupying the city seized the house as property of an absent rebel.

In March 1864, the house briefly served as the executive mansion of the newly elected governor of Louisiana, Michael Hahn. It then became the residence of Maj. Gen. Nathaniel P. Banks, U.S. Commander, Department of the Gulf.

The house was returned to Colonel Short by the United States government on August 15, 1865, and he lived in it until his death in 1890.

An addition was made in 1906 and the house was restored in 1950.

The unusual cast-iron morning glory and cornstalk fence was furnished by the Philadelphia Foundry of Wood and Perot.

The present owners are Mr. and Mrs. Thomas B. Favrot.

Domingos House
2703 Camp Street

Built in the 1850s, this delightful residence is a typical Greek Revival raised cottage with a side hall. It has a recessed gallery that spans the width of the house. A cast-iron railing connects the four simple, square columns that support a deep entablature embellished with a dentil course and a parapet. The windows facing the gallery are from floor to ceiling.

Because of its durability and suitability to the humid New Orleans climate, cypress was the only wood used in the construction of this well-preserved house.

Mr. and Mrs. K. Kirk Domingos III acquired ownership in September 1992. They take great pleasure in maintaining their home and their lovely garden.

Transom with hinges on the side instead of the top.

In the sunny parlor one finds an antique Victorian sofa that originally belonged to Mr. Domingos' great-grandmother. The faux marble of the original cypress mantelpiece was designed by Grace Newburger.

In the dining room, the table is set with Limoges china. Chippendale chairs sur-round the Queen Anne table on the gleaming cypress wood floor.

The kitchen table and chairs are of mahogany, and the mantelpiece is of cypress.

In the hallway stands an armoire dating back to 1850. It was made in Louisiana. The staircase has a mahogany railing and a simple but elegant newel-post.

A view of the enchanting garden, which has old-fashioned English roses as well as other colorful flowers.

Commander's Palace Tower
1403 Washington Avenue

The tower at Commander's Palace, one of the most notable of New Orleans' restaurants, reaches majestically toward the sky. This restaurant has been a New Orleans landmark since 1880. The award-winning quality of the food draws out-of-town visitors as well as diners from the entire New Orleans area. It is, indeed, a favorite of the Garden District residents.

There are many spacious, beautifully appointed, welcoming dining rooms in this Victorian fantasy of a building.

Lafayette Cemetery No. 1
1400 Washington Avenue

An impressive cast-iron entrance gate leads into this cemetery, which was laid out by Benjamin Buisson, city surveyor, in 1833 when the square was acquired by the City of Lafayette from Cornelius Hurst.

Among the many historic tombs are those of Samuel Jarvis Peters, originator of the New Orleans public school system, and Gen. Harry T. Hays, who gave distinguished service in the Confederate armed forces. Many residents of German and Irish descent who lived in the City of Lafayette are buried here.

Burial vaults form the cemetery wall along Washington Avenue. These were restored and the magnolia trees were replanted by the City of New Orleans in 1970.

A bas-relief of a fire fighters' vehicle appears at the top of the fire fighters' tomb.

The tomb for fire fighters who lost their lives has multiple vaults.

Part of the elaborately designed cast-iron fence surrounding the tomb.

Christ Church Cathedral
2901 St. Charles Avenue

Shortly after the Louisiana Purchase, the first local congregation of the Episcopal church was established and on November 17, 1805, its first service was held in the Cabildo.

In 1815 Henry S. Latrobe, architect, designed an octagonal Gothic church, which was erected at Canal and Bourbon streets. It was replaced in 1835 by a Greek Revival church. The design for this church was by Gallier and Dakin, a prestigious architectural firm. In 1846, a third Episcopal church was erected in Gothic style at Canal and Dauphine streets by Thomas K. Wharton, architect, and James Gallier, Sr., architect and builder. In 1886 the present elaborate, Gothic-style church on St. Charles Avenue was built. It was designed by Lawrence B. Valk of New York, architect, and Benjamin M. Harrod of New Orleans, supervising architect.

The Right Reverend Leonidas Polk, D.D., first bishop of Louisiana, and a general in the Confederate States Army, died in battle during the Civil War and is entombed in the south choir aisle of this magnificent structure.

An overall view of the splendid interior of Christ Church Cathedral.

Dominique Stella House
2915 Chestnut Street

In 1867, Dominique Stella commissioned Frederick Wing, architect, to draw the plans for this stately mansion. It was designed in an architectural blend of columned Greek Revival and Italianate styles.

The interior is exquisitely furnished in eighteenth-century English antiques, Oriental carpets, and seventeenth-, eighteenth-, and nineteenth-century art. Crystal chandeliers hang from beautiful medallions in the high-ceilinged, spacious rooms. The large garden room opens onto the terrace and gardens.

This home is maintained with loving care by the present owners.

The entrance hallway features an elegant staircase.

Through an exquisitely carved arch one sees the double parlor with twin crystal chandeliers.

The master bedroom, with an antique bed and chandelier.

A bright, sunny corner of the garden room.

On the terrace one finds a pleasant sitting area with charming statuary.

McDermott-Laborde House
2926 St. Charles Avenue

The original owner, Thomas McDermott, commissioned this lovely old Southern home to be built by an unknown architect, in 1882; however, it was designed in the style of homes constructed in the 1860s. It was the McDermott residence for many years.

Several changes in ownership took place throughout the years until Mr. and Mrs. George Coiron acquired it in 1964. During extensive restoration the Coirons discovered that year-round interior comfort was assured by the original designer, who left air space between the inner and outer walls, which are twelve inches apart, thereby keeping the house cooler in summer and warmer in winter.

The current owners are Mr. and Mrs. E. Theodore Laborde, who carefully maintain this beautiful home, which they purchased in January 1993.

Close-up of the beautiful fluted columns supporting the second-floor gallery.

The double parlor has twin mantelpieces.

Lovely light streams through the undraped floor-to-ceiling windows. To the right stands an antique armoire.

The open iron gate invites one into the rear garden.

AT LEFT: *The cypress wood stairway is elegant in its simplicity. The rear door of the entrance hall is surrounded by faux marble created by Charles Richardson, artist. The bust at the top of the door is a flat painting that appears to be three dimensional. This is called "trompe l'oeil."*

Van Benthuysen-Elms Mansion
3029 St. Charles Avenue

In 1869 Lewis E. Reynolds, architect, directed the construction of this grand Italianate mansion for "Yankee in Grey," Capt. Watson Van Benthuysen II, C.S.A. He was a relative by marriage of Jefferson Davis and quartermaster of the presidential convoy that fled Richmond in April 1865.

Captain Van Benthuysen, originally from Brooklyn, New York, moved his family to New Orleans in the 1840s and eventually became an officer in the Confederate army. After the Civil War he became a merchant and an industrialist until he died in 1901.

The house served as the German Consulate and in 1951 was purchased by John Elms.

The grand staircase from the entrance foyer, free-standing with a hand-carved newel-post.

Dome at the top of the winding staircase.

Note the drawing room's antique furniture, the cornice carving, and the splendid ceiling design.

Another view of the drawing room featuring the imported Louis XVI mantelpiece of hand-carved Carrara marble, and the French beveled mirror above it.

All woodwork in the Empire Room is mahogany. Moldings and sconces are twenty-four-carat gold.

The dining room's elaborate mantelpiece rises to ceiling height with carved panels and caryatids. The crystal chandelier is imported.

Beautifully landscaped gardens and a columned summerhouse add to the charm of the mansion.

George Washington Cable House
1313 Eighth Street

In 1874 this simple but elegant house was built for George Washington Cable, a noted author who was an early advocate of civil rights for blacks. His books, *Old Creole Days* and *Strange True Stories of Louisiana,* earned him international fame.

In this home Cable reared his family and entertained his literary friends, such as Mark Twain, Joel Chandler Harris, Lafcadio Hearn, and Oscar Wilde.

Thomas N. Bernard House
1328 Harmony Street

The architectural style of the Bernard house is typical of early Louisiana raised cottages. The recessed entrance door gives access to a wide central hall, which is flanked by spacious rooms. The front gallery spans the width of the house and is reached by a long flight of steps. On each side of the entrance door are two symmetrically placed floor to ceiling windows.

This home is noted for its elegant simplicity.

Morris Mansion
St. Charles Avenue

Originally, a cottage was built on this property in the 1860s. In 1888 the cottage and the land, which extended to Carondelet Street, were sold to Mrs. John Morris, who commissioned Mr. Thomas Sully, eminent architect, to build the present house. Mrs. Morris, however, was superstitious about totally demolishing the cottage; therefore, she had everything demolished except the living room, to which the rest of the magnificent mansion was added.

Mrs. Morris sold the house during the 1890s to Mr. and Mrs. Robert Moore, parents of Leila Moore who later married Kemper Williams. Leila and Kemper Williams were philanthropists who helped in furthering the dignity and growth of this historic city.

Robert Henry Downman bought the house in 1906 and became Rex, king of Mardi Gras, in 1907. Every year since then, Rex always stops the parade here so that he can offer a toast. Mr. Downman designed much of the interior millwork, fireplaces, and beams.

This room is radiant with the warm, glowing light of the sun. The beamed ceiling and the stained-glass windows are spectacular.

Close-up view of a stained-glass window.

The entrance hall with a mirrored wall and a marble-topped console table.

This view of the entrance hall shows the magnificent millwork.

This peaceful atmosphere invites one to relax. Note the magnificent wall covering.

The living room features an antique rug, an exceptional mantelpiece, and an antique piano.

Stewart House
Philip Street

Luther Wilson Stewart, a prosperous cotton broker, was the original owner of this classic Greek Revival mansion, which is typical of many antebellum homes.

The third owner, Charles Simon, remodeled the house from Greek Revival to Queen Anne/Victorian style. It then changed ownership several times.

In 1970 Monroe F. Labouisse III, noted architect, was commissioned to restore and remodel this lovely home to reflect the original Greek Revival style. Mr. Labouisse won an architectural award for this meticulous enterprise.

The present owners continue to maintain this beautifully restored home.

The double parlor has identical black marble, Greek, key-design mantelpieces. A Regency library table, with a Chinese equestrian figure and an inlaid top, stands next to the mantel in the front parlor.

150

There is a collection of Oriental rugs over polished pine flooring throughout the house. In the entrance hall, through a beautiful arch, one sees a Regency console table with an antique French mirror above it. A Chinese equestrian figure and antique Chinese porcelain grace this table.

The butler's pantry features a collection of faience (pottery), and a Romantic-Victorian-style marble-topped sideboard of mahogany.

The library is furnished with a collection of English Victorian and contemporary pieces. On the wall are portraits of the owners' children by Gene Seidenberg, artist, and other art by Louisiana contemporary artists.

A view of the lawn area of the garden through the fan-light window in the breakfast room. Around the table are bentwood chairs.

In the dining room an antique Empire mirror hangs over a George III English buffet. The Louisiana side tables are ca. 1830.

Alfred Grima House
St. Charles Avenue

Along tree-lined, historic St. Charles Avenue stands the Alfred Grima House, which was built about 1857 by Cornelius Bickwell Payne. In 1861 it was sold to Thomas L. Clarke. Alfred Grima acquired the mansion from Clarke in 1890 and had it completely remodeled within a year by Paul Andry and John McNally.

In 1925, the lovely formal garden was completed by Charles R. Armstrong.

Upon her death in 1981, Clarisse Claiborne Grima, widow of Alfred Grima, Jr., bequeathed the house to the Historic New Orleans Collection.

This magnificent home was acquired by private ownership in 1987.

A gracefully curved stairway, with an unusual newel-post, gives access to the upstairs rooms.

The entrance hallway as seen from the rear, featuring a charming antique chandelier and mirror. Note the singular cornice of simulated marble.

Against the far wall stands a magnificent American high chest. Note the marble mantelpiece and Italian mirror above it.

In the dining room one finds a two-part Queen Anne table with Chippendale chairs. The rug is Oriental.

French doors give an inviting view of the garden.

The patio is paved with bricks, enhancing the beauty of the captivating garden.

This is the strikingly lovely formal garden at Grima House.

Selected Bibliography

Federal Writers Project of the Works Progress Administration. *New Orleans City Guide.* Boston: Houghton Mifflin Co., 1938.

Huber, Leonard V. *Landmarks of New Orleans.* New Orleans: Louisiana Landmarks Society and Orleans Parish Landmarks Commission, 1984.

New Orleans Chapter of American Institute of Architecture. *A Guide to New Orleans Architecture.* New Orleans: New Orleans Chapter of American Institute of Architecture, 1974.

Samuel, Martha Ann Brett, and Ray Samuel. *The Great Days of the Garden District and the Old City of Lafayette.* New Orleans: Parents League of the Louise S. McGehee School, 1961.

Wilson, Samuel, Jr. *A Guide to Architecture of New Orleans, 1699-1959.* New York: Reinhold Publishing Corp., 1959.